The Let's Talk Library™

Let's Talk About Going to a Funeral

Marianne Johnston

The Rosen Publishing Group's
PowerKids Press™
New York

Special thanks to Vay-Schleich and Meeson Funeral Home, Inc., in Rochester, New York, for help in acquiring photographs.

Published in 1997 by The Rosen Publishing Group, Inc.
29 East 21st Street, New York, NY 10010

First Edition

Book Design: Erin McKenna

Photo Illustrations: Cover by Carrie Ann Grippo; p. 16 by Suzanne Sonsky; all photo illustrations by Carrie Ann Grippo.

Johnston, Marianne.
    Let's talk about going to a funeral / Marianne Johnston.
        p.   cm. — (Let's talk library)
    Includes index.
    Summary: Gives an overview of what a funeral is, why our culture holds them, and what might happen at one.
    ISBN 0-8239-5038-7
    1. Funeral rites and ceremonies—United States—Juvenile literature. [1. Funeral rites and ceremonies. 2. Death. 3. Grief.] I. Title. II. Series.
    GT3203.A2J64 1996
    393'.9—dc20
                                             96-46003
                                               CIP
                                             AC

Manufactured in the United States of America

Table of Contents

What Is a Funeral?

Everyone will die at some time. Like animals and plants, people usually die when they are old. Most people live for a long time. When someone dies, it may be a sad, confusing, and scary time for that person's family and friends. A **funeral** (FYOO-ner-ul) is a special ceremony that makes the death easier for family and friends to accept.

◀ All living things die at some time.

5

Why Have a Funeral?

A funeral is a time for all the people who loved the person who died to share their sadness with each other. It is important to let that sadness out instead of keeping it inside.

A funeral is also a time to **honor** (ON-er) the person who died. People can take time to remember that person's life.

Funerals help people learn to accept that someone they love is gone from their lives. ▶

What Happens at a Funeral?

Funerals are usually held in a religious place, such as a church or temple. Sometimes they are held at a place called a funeral home. People going to a funeral usually wear formal, dark-colored clothes to show respect for the person who died. Once everyone is seated, the minister or rabbi begins to speak. He or she may say a prayer and talk about the person who died. You may hear music. After the prayers and songs, a **eulogy** (YOO-luh-jee) is given. This is when a family member or friend talks about the life of the person who died.

◀ Funerals are a sad time for everyone.

When You First Get There

At a funeral, you may notice a big box made of wood or metal. This is called a **coffin** (KOF-in). The body of the person who died is kept in the coffin. At some funerals, the coffin is open. This is so family and friends can see the person who died one more time. Many people gently touch or kiss the body. You can do that if you want to. But you don't have to. The person who died will look different from the last time you saw him or her. It will look sort of like the person is asleep.

Some coffins are made of wood. ▶
Others are made of metal.

Grieving

People often cry at funerals. Don't be scared if you see your mom or dad or other grown-ups cry. Crying is a part of **grieving** (GREE-ving). Grieving means accepting that a special person has died and is gone from your life. Grieving helps your body and mind sort through the sad, confusing feelings that happen when someone dies. At a funeral, you grieve with others. Sharing your pain helps it go away faster than keeping it to yourself.

◀ Many people cry at funerals. Crying helps them feel better.

13

The Funeral Procession

When the service is over, **pallbearers** (PAWL-BAYR-erz) carry the coffin out of the church or temple. The pallbearers are usually family members or close friends of the person who died. They place the coffin in a long, black car called a **hearse** (HERSS). Everyone at the funeral gets into their own cars and follows the hearse to the **cemetery** (SEM-ih-ter-ee). This is called the funeral **procession** (pro-SEH-shun). Sometimes a police officer rides next to the line of cars to make sure everyone gets to the cemetery okay.

14

The hearse is a special car that ▶
carries coffins to cemeteries.

The Cemetery

A cemetery is a big, grassy place where people who have died are buried. You will probably see many **gravestones** (GRAYV-stohnz). These mark the places where people who have died are buried. Usually the names of the people and the dates that they died are carved on the gravestones. Some gravestones are very fancy. Others are plain and simple.

◀ Cemeteries are usually quiet, peaceful places.

At the Grave

A **grave** (GRAYV) is a place where a person who has died is buried. It is a hole about six feet deep. Once everyone arrives at the grave, the pallbearers carry the coffin to the grave. The minister or rabbi says a few more words. Sometimes people put roses or other flowers on the coffin. Everyone gathers around the grave while the coffin is lowered into the hole. When everyone is gone, the hole is filled in again.

Many people visit the grave of someone they love on birthdays or holidays. ▶

Cremation

Not all people who die are buried. Some people choose to be **cremated** (CREE-may-tid). This is when the body is burned in a place called a **crematorium** (cree-mah-TOR-ee-um). After the body is cremated, there are ashes. The ashes are usually placed in a small container called an **urn** (ERN). Some families keep the urn in their homes. Others bury it in a cemetery. Still others spread the ashes of the person who died in a special place, such as the ocean or in a garden.

◄ Some urns are fancy, like this one.
Others are very simple.

After the Funeral

Some families don't want to be alone after a funeral. People usually gather together at someone's house after a funeral. There is often lots of food at the gathering. Some people cry, some talk, and some even laugh. Some people tell stories about the person who died. Others sit quietly, thinking about that person. These are all normal reactions to the death of someone you love. Everyone is trying to learn to live without that person. Talking about that person makes accepting his or her death a little easier.

Glossary

cemetery (SEM-ih-ter-ee) A place where people who have died are buried.

coffin (KOF-in) A box in which a person who has died is buried.

cremate (CREE-mayt) Burning the body of a person who has died.

crematorium (cree-mah-TOR-ee-um) Place in which bodies of people who have died are burned.

eulogy (YOO-luh-jee) A speech given at a funeral about the life of the person who has died.

funeral (FYOO-ner-ul) A ceremony held at the burial of a person who has died.

grave (GRAYV) A place in which a person who has died is buried.

gravestone (GRAYV-stohn) A stone marker of a grave.

grieving (GREE-ving) Learning how to accept the death of someone.

hearse (HERSS) A special car that carries a coffin to the cemetery.

honor (ON-er) To show respect to.

pallbearer (PAWL-BAYR-er) A person who helps carry a coffin.

procession (pro-SEH-shun) People walking or driving slowly in a line.

urn (ERN) A container that holds the ashes of the body of someone who has died.

Index